I-SPY

with David Bellamy

NIGHT SKY

I-Spy Books
12 Star Road, Partridge Green
Horsham, Sussex RH13 8RA

For most of us the stars are no more than fascinating far away things, and though space travel may one day take you to the planets in our solar system, it is unlikely that we will ever reach the stars. If we did we would, of course, be in trouble, for like our sun they are gigantic thermo-nuclear reactors.

A good way of starting on the road to becoming an astronomer is to visit a planetarium. The cover picture shows the London Planetarium, about which there is more information in the Membership Book (see page 47).

The planetarium instrument projects pictures of the sun, moon, stars, planets and even space ships and satellites, on the inside surface of a huge hollow dome. Under the dome you can sit in perfect comfort, and learn about the positions and movements of the stars and planets – not only now, but in the past or future.

FOREWORD

I wonder if you have ever looked up into the sky and tried to understand what you can see there? Probably you have – but at first sight the stars look just like each other. This is not really true. There are stars of all kinds, some red, some white; there are even some stars which look obviously blue. Then there are the planets – worlds like our own Earth, which move around from one star-group into another. The Moon shows its monthly changes of shape, and you can see the dark patches on it which we call 'seas' even though there is no water in them.

The sky becomes so much more interesting when you know just what is there. This book will help you to make a start. So – go out 'spying', and you will have tremendous fun. I wish you all success.

PATRICK MOORE

GOLDEN RULES OF NIGHT I-SPYING

You will be able to see a lot from the bottom of your garden (please not from your bedroom window). But you will get the best views in the long winter nights and out in the country and seaside, far away from the glare of town lights.

1. Always tell your parents (it is a good excuse for staying up late, very educational).

2. Try to get them or your elder brother or sister to come with you.

3. Always wear warm clothes, a shivering astronomer wobbles the telescope.

I-SPY a **telescope** mounted on a stand so that it can be swivelled round and upwards for searching the heavens.

A red-letter day for you when you can

explore the sky through one of these!
I-SPYed one at .... Score **25**

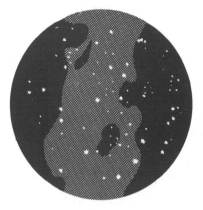

THE MILKY WAY

Before telescopes were invented, many stories were told to account for the silver path in the heavens that we call the MILKY WAY. You will see it stretching from horizon to horizon in a clear night sky. Its dim light comes from countless thousands of stars, millions of millions of miles out in space.

I-Spyed the Milky Way on ....
The time was ....
I was at ....
.... Score **20**

Light travels at 299,792 kilometres per second.
How far will it travel in a minute? ....
.... Score **30**

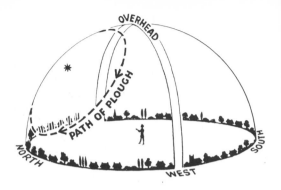

THE STAR WHEEL

Although the stars are really dotted about all over the space, you can imagine that they are painted on the inside of a huge dome and that you are standing underneath – where the little figure is in the picture – with the horizon all round you.

The North Star is rather like the hub of a giant wheel – it stays in almost the same position while all the other stars turn round it once every 24 hours. The dotted circle in the picture shows the path followed by the Plough. It never dips below the horizon because it is close to the North Star.

Look at page 9 and you will see that on the map there, the dome picture is drawn flat, with most of the southern sky left out.

5000 stars can be seen with the naked eye on a clear night.

6

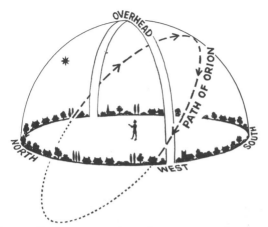

Constellations are imaginary groupings of stars invented by people to help them map the sky. They are still the easiest way to learn the stars.

The picture above shows the path of a constellation – such as Orion – which is further away from the North Star. You can see that it rises in the east, swings up into the southern half of the sky, and then sets below the western horizon twelve hours later.

Compare this picture with the map on page 27. You will understand the map more easily if you hold it over your head, with north on the map pointing towards north. You will then be in the same position as the little figure in the picture above – looking up towards the stars overhead, with the western horizon on your left, the eastern horizon on your right, and south behind you.

THE NORTHERN SKY

You will easily spot the **Plough**, a group of seven stars in the shape of a plough. I reckon it looks more like a saucepan.

The two end stars are called the 'pointers' because a line drawn through them points towards the **North Star**, see below.

I-SPYed the Plough on ....

From where? .... Score **20**

I-SPYed the North Star on ....

From where? .... Score **20**

The Plough is part of a constellation called the **Great Bear**. Below on the right is how it used to be drawn.

Which part is the Plough? ....

.... Score **5**

I-SPYed the Great Bear on ....

From where? .... Score **20**

The chart on the next page shows the Great Bear in four different positions.

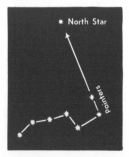

With a pair of binoculars you can see more than two million stars.

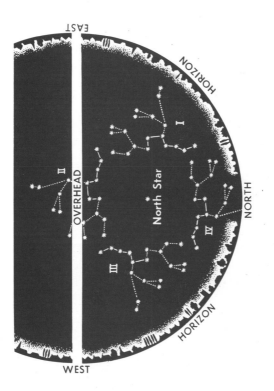

Which position was the Great Bear nearest to when you saw it? I, II, III or IV ....
....

Little Bear is in the sky, too. Below on the left is how it used to be drawn on the old star maps.

I-SPY that the North Star – the brightest star in this constellation – is at the tip of the bear's 'tail'.

The map on the right shows the position of the Little Bear and The Plough.

I-SPYED the Little Bear on ....

The time was ....

I was at ....

.... Score **20**

In the pictures on the opposite page, you can see how the Little Bear goes round the North Star – almost as if he is being swung round the sky by his tail!

The heaviest stars are the brightest (they may look faint because they are a long way away) and the highest in temperature.

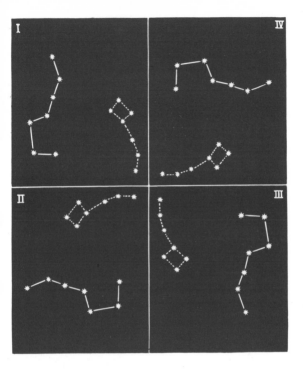

Which position was the Little Bear nearest to when you saw it? I, II, III or IV ....
....
....

The sun travels towards Hercules and Lyra at a speed of a million miles a day.

HERCULES AND THE DRAGON

You can see below on the left how the Greek hero **Hercules** used to be shown, with the stars on the **Dragon** under his foot.

The other map shows the Dragon, Hercules, the Little Bear and the Plough.

I-SPYed the Dragon on ....
The time was ....
The place was ....
.... Score **30**
I-SPYed Hercules on ....
The time was ....
The place was ....
.... Score **30**

Look at the picture on page 13 and you will see the path Hercules follows, rising in the north-east and setting in the north-west.

The Dragon is closer to the North Star and never sets.

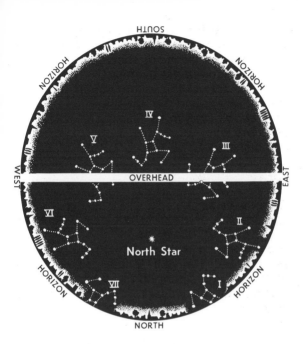

Which position was Hercules nearest to when you saw it? I, II, III, IV, V, VI or VII ......

....

....

Make your own drawing or painting of Hercules and the Dragon with the stars inside – score an extra 20 for each.

An orrery is a working model of the solar system, the planets can be moved round the sun at their correct velocities. Score 100 if you see one.

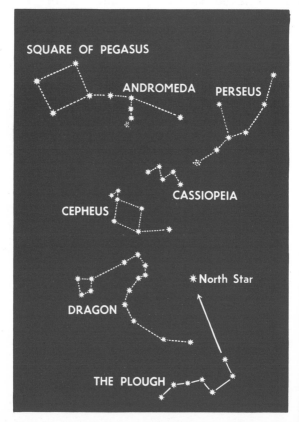

A LEGEND IN THE SKY

I-SPY in the map on the opposite page the constellation of **Perseus**. The picture below shows how this group was drawn by the old map artists. The Greek hero is holding the snake-haired head of the Medusa in his left hand.

Do you know the story of how Perseus came up on his winged sandals and rescued the princess who had been chained to a rock?

On the next two pages you can see other characters from Greek legends.

Find the story in a book if you don't know it
.... Score **30**
I-SPYed Perseus on ....
The time was ....
I was at .... Score **30**

15

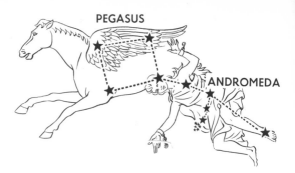

PEGASUS

ANDROMEDA

This picture is upside down to show how the horse fits in.

PEGASUS AND ANDROMEDA

Here are Pegasus, the winged horse, who carried Bellerophon in his expedition against a nasty fire-breathing dragon, and Princess Andromeda. I-SPY in this picture and in the map on page 14, that **Andromeda** and the **Square of Pegasus** make a star group that looks something like a very big Plough.

Look through the star maps on page 33 to 40 and you will be able to follow these constellations as they swing round the sky.

I-SPYed Andromeda on ....

....

From ....

.... Score **30**

I-SPYed the Square of Pegasus on ....

....

From ....

.... Score **30**

THE KING AND QUEEN

I-SPY below left the constellation of **Cepheus**
Andromeda's father.

This group is quite close to the North Star
– as you can see from the map on page 14 –
and so it never sets.

I-SPYed Cepheus on ....
....
From .... Score **30**

Cassiopeia, the Queen, is easy to identify. It
forms a W – or an M if it is seen the other way
up! – on the Milky Way.

This is how Cassiopeia used to be drawn –
as a lady in a chair.

I-SPYed Cassiopeia on ....
From ....
.... Score **30**

THE STAR SWAN

I-SPY the constellation of **Cygnus**. It is the Latin word for swan.

The five stars of this group form a cross (sometimes called the Northern Cross). The brightest star, **Deneb**, is the 'tail' and the side-arms of the cross represent the outstretched wings of a big bird in flight. Find Cygnus by starting from the North Star and following a curved line through Cepheus to the Milky Way.

I-SPYed Cygnus on ....
From .... Score **30**
I-SPYed Deneb on ....
From .... Score **20**

The map opposite shows the path the Swan follows round the North Star. At its highest point it is overhead and just in the southern half of the sky.

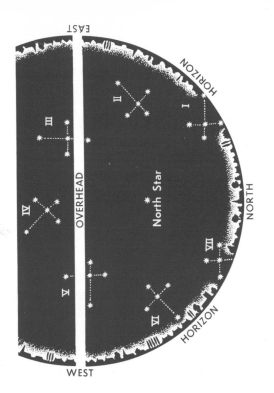

Which position was the Swan nearest to when you saw it? I, II, III, IV, V, VI or VII ......

....

THE HERDSMAN AND THE CROWN

Follow the curve of the Plough's 'handle' and you will see that it points towards the constellation called the **Herdsman**. The very bright star in this group is called **Arcturus**.

Between the Herdsman and Hercules is a small C-shaped constellation. This is the **Crown**.

I-SPYed the Herdsman on ....
From .... Score **40**
I-SPYed Arcturus on ....
From .... Score **20**
I-SPYed the Crown on ....
From .... Score **20**

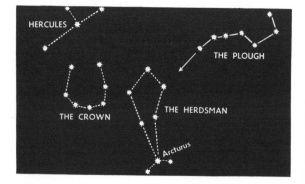

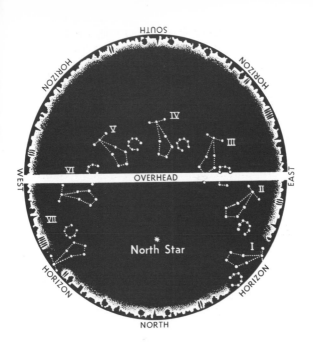

Which position were the Herdsman and Crown nearest to when you saw them?
I, II, III, IV, V, VI or VII ....
....

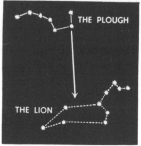

THE LION IN THE SKY

I-SPY the constellation of **Leo** the Latin word for lion. On the left is how the old star maps showed it.

Follow the line of the Plough's pointers away from the North Star and you will find Leo — but if you are facing North you will have to turn round to see it.

Do you think that this group looks like a lion? Remember, you may not see it the 'right way up' as it is in the picture here.

The map on the opposite page shows how Leo follows a path that takes him well into the southern half of the sky.

I-SPYed Leo on ....

The time was ....

I was at ....

.... Score **40**

The Zodiac means 'Path of Creatures', an ancient name for the belt in the sky within which the moon and chief planets are always found.

The signs of the Zodiac were probably connected with the twelve ancient months and seasons of the year. Leo is the fifth sign of the Zodiac and is best seen from February to the end of June.

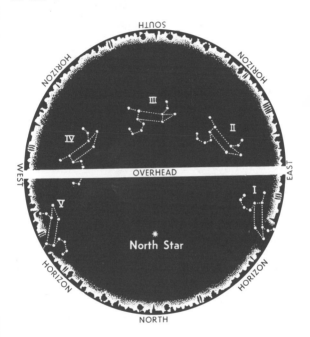

Which position was Leo nearest to when you saw it? I, II, III, IV or V ....
...
...

THE CRAB AND THE TWINS

I-SPY the **Crab**, a group of rather faint stars right under the Lion's 'nose'. A little further away from Leo is the constellation of the **Heavenly Twins**. The brightest stars in this group are **Castor** and **Pollux**.

I-SPYed the Crab from ....

.... Score **40**

I-SPYed the Heavenly Twins from ....

.... Score **40**

I-SPYed Castor on ....

.... Score **20**

I-SPYed Pollux on ....

.... Score **20**

In the centre of the stars that make up the lion's head, Meteor showers can be seen in November but only after midnight when Leo rises.

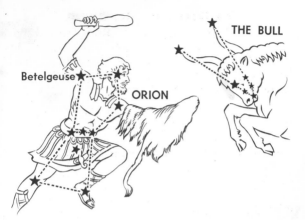

Betelgeuse · ORION · THE BULL

THE HUNTER AND THE BULL

This rather dramatic picture shows how the constellations of **Orion** the Hunter and **Taurus** the Bull were drawn on the old maps. I-SPY the three stars in a line forming Orion's Belt, and **Betelgeuse**, the large star at Orion's 'shoulder'.

The map on the next page will help you to find these groups and the picture on page 27 shows the path Orion follows through the sky. *Score for these over the page.*

Betelgeuse is 650 light years away from Earth. *How many kilometres is that? (Clue: see page 30)* .... Score **50**

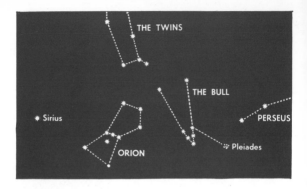

I-SPY **Sirius,** the brightest star in the night sky. Its name means 'shining one'. A line through the three stars of Orion's belt points roughly towards Sirius.

I-SPYed Orion on ....
.... Score **50**
I-SPYed Taurus on ....
.... Score **40**
I-SPYed Orion's Belt on ....
.... Score **20**
I-SPYed Betelgeuse on ....
.... Score **20**
I-SPYed Sirius on ....
.... Score **50**

Which position was Orion nearest to when you saw it? I, II, III, IV or V ....

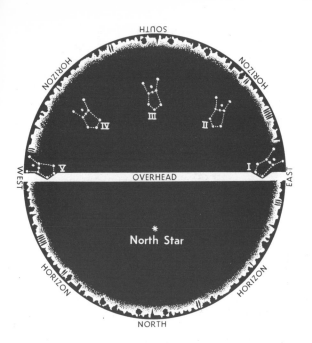

SATELLITES

There are now many artificial satellites orbiting the Earth. These reflect the light just like our own moon and may be identified as pin points of light moving across the sky.

When did you see your satellite? ....
.... Score **30**
If you saw it on two nights running score 20 more.

THE CHARIOTEER

I-SPY left the constellation called the **Charioteer** between Perseus and the Heavenly Twins.

The brightest star in this group is called **Capella**.

I-SPYed the Charioteer on ....
.... Score **25**
I-SPYed Capella on ....
.... Score **15**
I-SPYed Lyra on ....
.... Score **25**
I-SPYed Vega on ....
.... Score **15**

THE LYRE

Lyra, or the Lyre, is a small constellation lying between Hercules and the Swan.

Vega is a brilliant star that shines with a bluish-white light.

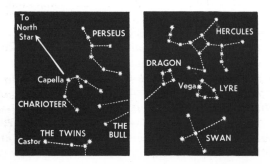

28

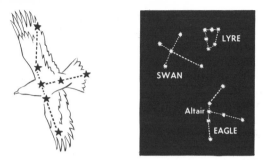

THE EAGLE IN THE SKY

The Swan will help you to find a group of stars named after a much fiercer bird. Look at the picture above and you will see that the neck of the flying Swan points roughly towards the **Eagle**.

The star **Altair** is much brighter than the others in the constellation of the Eagle.

The brightest stars – like Altair, Sirius, and Vega – are said to be of the first magnitude.

I-SPYed the Eagle on ....

From .... Score **30**

I-SPYed Altair on ....

From .... Score **20**

Vega was the Pole Star 14,000 years ago. Some temples built by the Egyptians had shafts down which it always shone. The position of the Pole Star changes 1° every 70 years, Vega will again be the Pole Star in another 12,000 years.

THE GREAT NEBULA

I-SPY the biggest and most distant thing I have ever seen.

In the constellation of Andromeda there is a tiny oval patch. It is the **Great Nebula**, an enormous cloud of dust and gas out of which stars form. Light travels at 9.45 million million kilometres per year, and yet it would take over 100,000 years for light to cross the Andromeda galaxy. That's how big it is. Whowee! Thousands of millions of galaxies make up the universe.

Some Nebulae, like the **Horsehead Nebula** shown (front cover), can be seen even without a telescope or binoculars. It is 1100 light years away. Choose a clear night and look for a hazy patch.

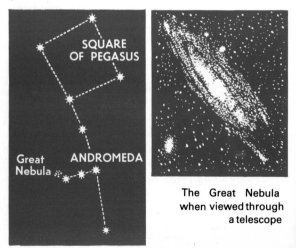

The Great Nebula when viewed through a telescope

I-SPYed the Great Nebula on ....
The time was ....
From .... Score **50**

A METEOR

Shooting stars – or Meteors – are not really stars at all. They are tiny particles that are burned up by friction as they rush through the upper atmosphere.

I-SPYed a Meteor on ....
The time was ....
....
At .... Score **30**

Some objects from space are large enough to reach the Earth before they burn away. You can see these Meteorites in many museums.

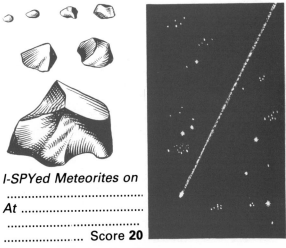

I-SPYed Meteorites on

....
At ....
....
.... Score **20**

STAR CLUSTERS

In the constellation of Taurus you will see a little cluster of stars called the **Pleiades**. They are sometimes called the Seven Sisters, although you can probably see only six.

The seventh star is not very clear but you should be able to see it. Try hard and then check with binoculars.

I-SPY below right another cluster – **Praesepe** – in the constellation of the Crab. It is rather more difficult to find than the Pleiades.

If you have forgotten how to find the Crab turn back to the map on page 24.

I-SPYed the Pleiades on ....

From .... Score **25**

I-SPYed Praesepe on ....

....

From .... Score **35**

....

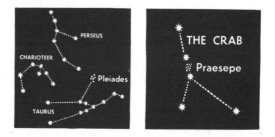

Stars of the Pleiades were 'born' 60 million years ago – very young by cosmic standards.

STAR MAPS

To use the star maps on these eight pages, first find the Plough in the sky. Decide which of the maps looks most like the night sky you are looking at, and then hold the map over your head – with north on the map pointing north. All the other directions will then be correct, and the stars on the map will be in the same positions as those in the sky.

STAR MAP 1

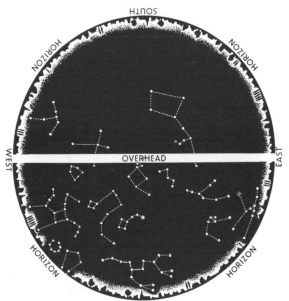

STAR MAP 2

I-SPY that when the Plough is in this position, Cassiopeia and Perseus are overhead and the Dragon is between the Little Bear and the northern horizon. The Heavenly Twins and Orion are just above the eastern horizon. The Swan and the Lyre are fairly low in the northwest.

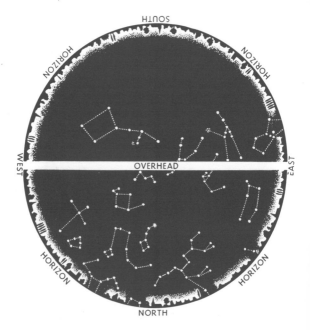

STAR MAP 3

I-SPY that when the Plough is in this position, the Charioteer and Perseus are overhead, the Crab and the Lion are over the eastern horizon, and the Swan is on the north-west horizon. Orion is to the south and the Square of Pegasus is in the west.

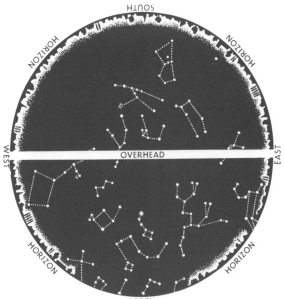

STAR MAP 4

I-SPY that when the Plough is in this position, the Herdsman and the Crown are on the north-eastern horizon, while Orion is low in the south-west. The Lion is high up in the east and the Crab towards the south. Perseus, Taurus, and the Charioteer are well up in the west.

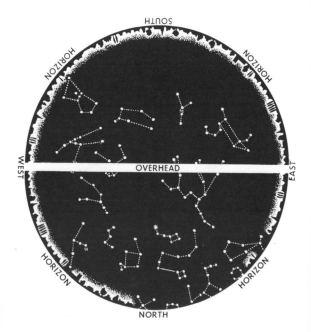

STAR MAP 5

I-SPY that when the Plough is directly above the North Star, the Lion is high up in the south, the Lyre and Hercules are above the north-eastern horizon, and the Twins are fairly low in the west. Cepheus and Cassiopeia are between the North Star and the northern horizon.

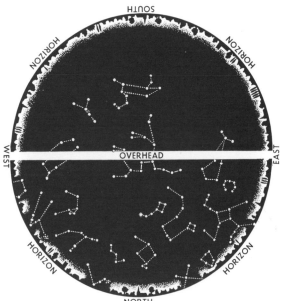

STAR MAP 6

I-SPY that when the Plough is in this position, the Herdsman is overhead and slightly to the south, and Hercules high in the east. The Lion and the Crab are low in the west.

The Lyre, the Swan, and Cepheus are well up over the north-eastern horizon. Cassiopeia is between the North Star and the horizon.

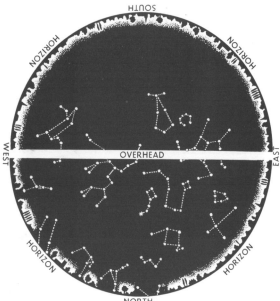

STAR MAP 7

I-SPY that when the Plough is in this position,
the Square of Pegasus and Andromeda are on
the north-eastern horizon. The Herdsman, the
Crown, Hercules and the Lyre are a little to the
south, and the Lion is on the western horizon.

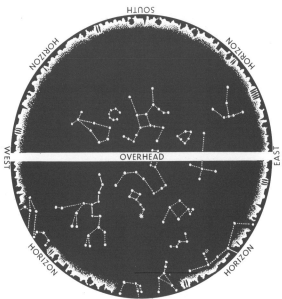

39

STAR MAP 8

I-SPY that when the Plough is in this position,
the Herdsman and Crown are fairly low in the
west. The Swan and the Lyre are just to the
south overhead and the Eagle well up in the
south. Pegasus and Andromeda are well above
the horizon in the east.

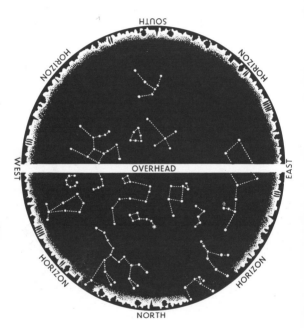

A RING ROUND THE MOON

I-SPY a **Corona** or a **Halo** – count your points for either – around the moon.

A halo is a huge circle of whitish light with a red tinge on the inside, caused by light from the moon passing through a thin cloud of ice crystals high up in the atmosphere.

A corona is a much smaller circle with a bluish tint on the inside of the ring and red on the outside.

Corona or Halo? ....

Where were you? ....

.... Score **50**

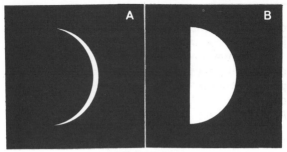

THE MOON

The Moon shines because it reflects sunlight. As it goes round the Earth it is lit first on one side, then full face, and then on the other side.

I-SPY the new moon (A). The picture on the left (B) shows the first quarter. One half of the moon is shining, but it has completed only one-quarter of its journey round the Earth.

The sun is shining from the right, so the left-hand side of the moon is in darkness.

I-SPYed	Date	Time	Place	Score
(A)				**20**
(B)				**20**

When you see the full moon (C) you know that the sun is behind the Earth and lighting up the whole face of the moon.

What was the name of the first person to set foot on the moon? ....

.... Score **30**

Later in the month you will see the last quarter (D), and then the waning crescent (E) just before sunrise.

If you want to know when to look for the different phases of the moon, you will probably find the dates in your diary or calendar.

I-SPYed (C) on .... Score **20**

....

I-SPYed (D) on .... Score **20**

....

I-SPYed (E) on .... Score **20**

....

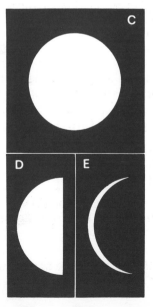

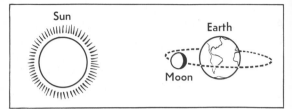

AN ECLIPSE OF THE SUN

The picture shows what happens when there is an **eclipse of the sun**. The moon comes to a point on its orbit, or path round the Earth, where it is directly between us and the sun, and we see the moon as a black disc on the sun's face.

THE WORLD'S SHADOW

This may have given early observers a clue that the Earth was round. The eclipse happens when the moon moves into the shadow of the Earth in space.

An eclipse of the moon is rare but more common than eclipses of the sun as seen from any one place. You can score for finding out any interesting fact about it.

What have you discovered? ....
....
....
.... Score **70**

Double score if you see one.

44

A PLANET

A star shines because it is white hot and giving out its own light. A planet has no light of its own — it shines only because it reflects sunlight. **Venus** – although it looks like a big, bright star – is really a planet, spinning round the sun like our own Earth. You will see that Venus does not twinkle like a star.

Venus has no fixed position like the constellations of stars but it is never very far from the sun. This means that it will be in the west in the evening (it is sometimes called the evening star) and in the east early in the morning.

There are lots of exciting things waiting to be discovered on other planets. Now, with space travel, who says an I-SPYer won't be the first young person to explore outer space and find out?

I-SPYed Venus on ....

The time was ....

I was at ....

.... Score **50**

AN OBSERVATORY

The Royal Greenwich Observatory was founded by King Charles II at Greenwich in London, but moved to the clearer skies of Sussex after the Second World War and is now based at Herstmonceux Castle. However, today's large and powerful optical telescopes need to be sited where the skies are even clearer than at Herstmonceux and where the Earth's atmosphere won't cause distortion and shimmering of a star's image. The Observatory's largest telescope, the Isaac Newton Telescope (above) has therefore been moved to a new international observatory on the Canary Island of La Palma, where together with other new large telescopes it will be able to make more discoveries.

JOIN THE I-SPY CLUB

- All you need to join the I-SPY Club is to buy a Membership Book which includes the secret codes. Ask at your bookshop or newsagent.

- Tell your friends about I-SPY. Invite them to join and form a Patrol with you.

- Collect all the I-SPY books – and you'll have a wonderful library of your own.

- Write to me about any interesting discoveries you make. You may win a prize! Remember to enclose a stamped addressed envelope for a reply.

*LOOK OUT FOR THESE I-SPY WITH
DAVID BELLAMY BOOKS*

AT THE AIRPORT
ARCHAEOLOGY
AT THE ART
  GALLERY
BIRDS AND
  REPTILES AT
  THE ZOO
BRITISH COINS
BRITISH WILDLIFE
CREEPY CRAWLIES
ON A CAR
  JOURNEY
CAR NUMBERS
CARS
CIVIL AIRCRAFT
DINOSAURS
FISH AND FISHING

GARDEN FLOWERS
  ALL THE YEAR
  ROUND
GARDEN BIRDS
MAMMALS AT THE
  ZOO
NIGHT SKY
ON A DAY AT THE
  SEASIDE
ON A FARM
ON A TRAIN
  JOURNEY
PETS
POND LIFE
SUPERMARKETS
TREES
WILD FLOWERS

AND MANY MORE TO COME

INDEX

Altair	29	Meteorites	31
Andromeda	16	Milky Way	5
Arcturus	20	Moon	42–43, 44
Betelgeuse	25, 26	Nebula, the Great	30
Capella	28	North Star	6, 8
Cassiopeia	17	Northern Sky	8
Castor	24	Observatory	46
Cepheus	17	Orion's belt	25–26
Charioteer, the	28	Orion, the Hunter	25–26
Constellation	7	Pegasus	16
Corona	41	Perseus	14–15
Crab, the	24	Planet	45
Crown, the	20	Planetarium	2
Cygnus	18	Pleiades	32
Deneb	18	Plough	6–8
Dragon	12	Pollux	24
Eagle, the	29	Praesepe	32
Eclipse (moon)	42	Satellites	27
Eclipse (sun)	44	Seven Sisters	32
Great Bear	8–9	Shooting stars	31
Halo	41	Sirius	26
Heavenly Twins	24	Star Clusters	32
Hercules	12–13	Star Maps	33–40
Herdsman, the	20	Star Wheel	6–7
Leo the Lion	22–23	Taurus the Bull	25
Little Bear	10–11	Vega	28
Lyra (the Lyre)	28	Venus	45
Meteor	31		

Acknowledgements

Cover illustrations: *Front*, Nebula 'Horsehead' (Royal Observatory, Edinburgh, © 1978) *Back*, Interior of dome, showing projector, Jupiter and moonscape (London Planetarium)

Photos: Inside front cover, Press-Tige Pictures; Page 46, Royal Greenwich Observatory, Herstmonceux.

Series Editor: Rose Hill

Published by Ravette Limited, 12 Star Road, Partridge Green, Horsham, Sussex RH13 8RA.

© Ravette Ltd., 1985

Typeset by Kalligraphics Ltd., Surrey.

Printed in Spain by Meteu Cromo, Spain

ISBN 0 906710 66 9